D1608754

AMAZING SCIENCE

TIDAL WAVES

AND OTHER

OCEAN WONDERS

Q.L. PEARCE
Illustrated by Mary Ann Fraser

Julian Messner

To Andrea

Acknowledgment

With thanks to Rimmon C. Fay, Ph.D., marine biologist for the Pacific Bio-Marine Laboratories, for his assistance and critical review of the manuscript.

Library of Congress Cataloging-in-Publication Data
Pearce, Q.L. (Querida Lee)
    Amazing science. Tidal waves and other ocean wonders / Q.L. Pearce ; illustrated by Mary Ann Fraser.
        p. cm.
    Bibliography: p.
    Includes index.
    Summary: Describes some of the biological and geological wonders found in the ocean depths, including electric creatures, poisonous fish, swimming reptiles, the longest mountain chain, and a river in the ocean.
    1. Marine biology—Juvenile literature. 2. Ocean—Juvenile literature.
[1. Marine biology. 2. Ocean.] I. Fraser, Mary Ann, ill. II. Title. III. Title: Tidal waves and other ocean wonders.
QH91.16.P42 1989   89-9355
574.92-dc20   CIP
                                                              AC
    ISBN 0-671-68532-5 (lib. bdg.)
    ISBN 0-671-68647-X (pbk.)

Text copyright © 1989 by RGA Publishing Group, Inc.
Illustrations copyright © 1989 by RGA Publishing Group, Inc.
All rights reserved including the right of
reproduction in whole or in part in any form.
Published by Julian Messner, a division of
Silver Burdett Press, Inc., Simon & Schuster, Inc.
Prentice Hall Bldg., Englewood Cliffs, NJ 07632.

JULIAN MESSNER and colophon are trademarks of
Simon & Schuster, Inc.
Manufactured in the United States of America.

Lib. ed.:   10 9 8 7 6 5 4 3 2 1
Paper ed.: 10 9 8 7 6 5 4 3 2 1

Contents

Our Water Planet

Water covers nearly three-quarters of the planet Earth. In fact, if Earth's surface were completely smooth with no valleys or mountains, it would be under an ocean two miles deep. Besides being the only true water planet in the solar system, Earth is also the only planet to support life as we know it. That life began in the seas and oceans more than three billion years ago–many millions of years before any creature set foot on dry land.

We depend on the oceans for many things other than for supporting life. For instance, the Earth's great bodies of water contribute to our generally mild climate. Water stores heat much better than air does, and sun-warmed ocean currents distribute this heat from the warm equatorial regions to the colder polar regions. Since the beginning of recorded history and probably before, the sea has also been an important source of food for mankind. Fishermen catch more than sixty million tons of fish and shellfish every year. Someday tides, waves, and currents may even be a clean, readily available source of energy.

There are many wonders hidden in the ocean depths. Have you ever heard of a mountain chain longer than the circumference of the Earth, or floating chunks of ice taller than a five-story building? Did you know there are fish that can walk or fly, and a lizard that grazes on seaweed? This book will introduce you to these and other amazing features of Earth's extraordinary oceans.

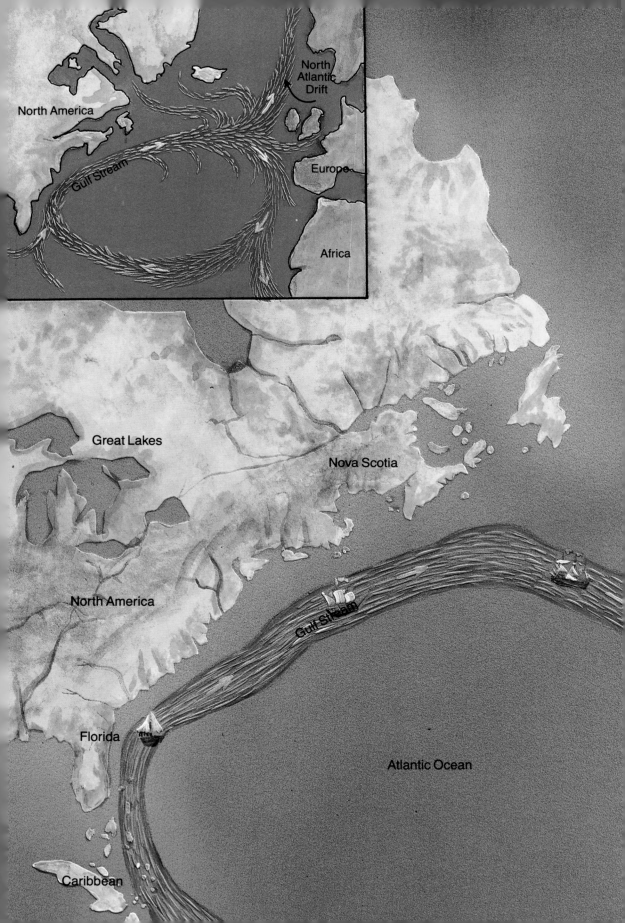

The Gulf Stream

There is a "river" in the Atlantic Ocean that carries more than 1,000 times the flow of the great Mississippi River. It is the Gulf Stream, the most powerful ocean current on Earth. It begins in the warm waters of the Florida Straits. At the narrowest part of the straits, the water flows up to seven miles per hour. That may not seem very fast to you, but that speed will take you out to sea rapidly.

The Gulf Stream is actually the western portion of a great circular movement of water in the North Atlantic Ocean. It flows northward along the eastern coast of the United States. As it passes Newfoundland, it flows out to sea toward northern Europe, where it becomes known as the North Atlantic Drift. Benjamin Franklin was the first to chart this path. As postmaster general in 1770, he noticed that the mail took two weeks longer to get from England to America than from America to England. He figured out that on the journey toward the colonies, the ships must be sailing against a very strong current.

The Gulf Stream warms the climates of Iceland and northern Europe. Warm air blowing inland from it actually keeps Reykjavik (RAYK·yah·vik), Iceland, warmer in winter than New York City, which is 2,400 miles farther south. Ben Franklin knew about the warming effect of the Gulf Stream. During the American Revolution, he studied the idea of changing its flow in order to plunge England into a little ice age. However, the plan wasn't very practical, and American independence was won without the help of the Gulf Stream.

The powerful, northward-flowing current of the Gulf Stream.

N. America

Europe

Atlantic Ocean

Sargasso Sea

Africa

S. America

Sargassum weed

crab

Sargassum fish

crab

Sargassum shrimp

The Sargasso Sea

In the early days of exploration, the Sargasso Sea had a bad reputation. Sailors told tales of ancient trading vessels, Spanish warships, and pirate ships trapped and rotting in the calm water. Seaweed was said to grow quickly over the ships, while sea monsters hid nearby to drag unlucky sailors to the bottom. The area was nicknamed "the graveyard of the sea."

Although it is not really a mysterious trap for ships, the Sargasso Sea is a unique place. Its warm, still, salty waters cover about two million square miles of the North Atlantic Ocean, an area more than half the size of the United States. Huge patches of rootless seaweed called sargassum, or gulfweed, drift on the surface. Clumps of tiny air-filled sacs keep the ruffly sargassum afloat.

Sea monsters may not lurk in the Sargasso Sea, but the animal life is quite incredible. Halobates (hel·AH·buh·teez), the only insect whose home is the open ocean, skitters across the surface of the water. Tiny crabs and sea horses cling to the weed, and various flying fish build their nests in it. The sargassumfish looks like the leafy surroundings of its seaweed home. Its colors match the seaweed and can change if its background changes. This little six-inch fish is not a strong swimmer, though. It hangs onto the sargassum with its tiny, jointed fins and pulls itself from branch to branch. It has a unique way of protecting itself. If swallowed, it sucks in water and swells up until its attacker must cough it up or choke.

The sargassumfish makes its home in the warm waters of the Sargasso Sea.

The Changing Tides

Hundreds of thousands of miles away in space, the silverly moon circles our planet. Did you know that this journey of the moon has a very important effect on the Earth? It is the most important factor affecting the tides of the Earth's waters. Each day, the sea level rises and falls as a result of the pull of the moon's gravity on our oceans. The difference in height between low and high tide is called the tidal range. A range of six to nine feet is not unusual along an average coastline, but in some places the difference between low and high tide is tremendous. The depth of the water and the shapes of the coastline and sea bed determine the tidal range.

The Bay of Fundy in Canada is world famous for its extraordinary tides. The tidal range there is at least fifty feet or more. That's as high as a five-story building. These remarkable tides cause another astonishing event, a reversing waterfall. At low tide the St. John River is a thundering waterfall that flows into the Bay of Fundy, passing through and over a narrow gorge. During this time, the water level is higher on the river side of the gorge than on the bay side. When the tide rises in the bay, however, water piles up very high at the mouth of the gorge and pours back into the river. This creates a reversed foaming waterfall, which lasts until the level of the river rises. As the tide ebbs, the thundering waterfall returns, but it falls in the other direction.

The extraordinary fifty-foot tidal range of the Bay of Fundy.

Tidal Waves

It may surprise you to learn that tidal waves are not caused by the tides. They are more accurately called *tsunamis* (soo·NAH·meez), a Japanese word for "large waves in harbor." It makes sense to use a Japanese word, because more than fifty of the waves have crashed on Japanese shores in the past seventy-five years. Tsunamis are caused by earthquakes, underwater avalanches, or volcanic eruptions. When one of these events occurs it can create "shock waves" that travel outward in ever-widening circles across the surface of the ocean. You can see the same rippling effect if you drop a pebble into a pail of water. In deep water, however, these waves can travel as fast as 600 miles per hour.

Tsunamis usually consist of eight waves. The third and the eighth are often the largest and most dangerous. As they near the shore, the water level usually drops, exposing the ocean floor. This happens so quickly that fish are stranded on the sand, until the water returns as a huge, rushing wall. Churning and hissing, it crashes over the shore, sweeping away everything in its path.

The greatest reported tidal wave occurred in 1883 after the explosion of a volcanic island named Krakatoa. The explosion was so violent that it was heard 3,000 miles away. That's as far as from San Francisco to New York City. As the island collapsed, a wave of water more than 120 feet high smashed into nearby islands, killing thousands of people. Many ships sank, but the giant wave snatched one gunboat from the ocean and carried it two miles inland.

*A crashing tsunami can destroy
a village in minutes.*

The Longest Mountain Chain

Did you know that there is a chain of mountains on Earth long enough to circle the globe nearly twice? Although this curving chain is some 40,000 miles long, and in some places more than 10,000 feet high, most people will never see more than the very top of one or two of the tallest peaks. That is because these mountains rise up from the great depth of the ocean floor.

Part of the steep, rugged chain rises in a long "S" shape in the middle of the Atlantic Ocean. It is called the Mid-Atlantic Ridge, and most of it lies at least a mile or two below sea level. Some of the tallest peaks form islands in the Atlantic Ocean, such as the Azores. A large section surfaces at the northern end as the huge island of Iceland.

There is a long ridge in the Indian Ocean, too. Like an upside-down "Y," it divides at its southern end. One branch curves around the tip of Africa and joins the Mid-Atlantic Ridge. The other branch curves around Australia to join the East Pacific Rise in the Pacific Ocean.

These incredible mountains are unlike any others on Earth. A deep gash called a rift cuts down into the center of many of the ridges. It is along this rift that new ocean floor is born. Hot rock, called magma, wells up from beneath the ocean floor and hardens. Then, as new crust forms, older crust on each side pushes away. This process, called seafloor spreading, adds about ten cubic miles of crust to our planet every year.

A great underwater chain of mountains–
where new ocean floor is born.

Underwater Chimneys

When most people think of the ocean depths, they picture dark, icy waters. Like the land, however, the ocean has many different environments. In the rift valleys of the Earth's great oceans, lava spews upward and hardens before reaching the ocean surface. Mounds and tubes as tall as 100 feet are formed. Scalding water and minerals flow from these long lava chimneys, nicknamed black or white smokers. Some scientists feel that as seawater seeps into cracks in the seafloor and is heated by the rock below, it spews from the chimneys at more than a million gallons per second! The water often contains chemicals and minerals that feed huge colonies of crimson-colored bacteria. The chemicals and bacteria alike are food for some very unusual animals.

When scientists investigated the first hot vents, they discovered thirty new animal species. In some places, huge, bright-red worms in long white tubes are attached to the surface of the lava rocks. These six-foot-long creatures have no mouth or gut. Instead, a special kind of bacteria living in the body of the worm helps to convert chemicals in the seawater to food. Huge, foot-long mussels with white shells and bright red meat compete with amazing giant clams for space near the underwater chimneys. Tiny, ghostly pale crabs scoot across the sandy bottom. They seem too fragile to survive the incredible water pressure at that depth, yet they will quickly die if raised to the lower pressure near the surface. Some animals around the hot vents are so odd that scientists are having a hard time classifying them. They are like nothing else on Earth.

A most unusual marine environment—
underwater lava chimneys.

Ancient Seas

The Earth's surface is a "thin" patchwork of plates floating on hot, fluid rock. As parts of these crustal plates, the continents go along for the ride. Scientists think that continents have been joining together and splitting apart for at least 500 million years, and that they originally looked nothing like they do today. Long ago, a huge sea of water separated the only two continents. This ancient sea contained many strange creatures, including the earliest ancestors of modern starfish and corals. Animals had not yet set foot on dry land.

About 250 million years ago, the continents crunched together to form one huge supercontinent called *Pangaea* (pan·GEE·uh), which in Greek means "all land." The first small dinosaurs scurried across this prehistoric landscape. Surrounding it was a huge sea called *Panthalassa* (pan·thuh·LASS·uh), or "all sea." Fifty million years later the lands began to split apart again, and the Atlantic Ocean was born. A huge body of water, the Sundance Sea, then spread across North America. Ferocious ancestors of today's shark probably swam over much of what is now Colorado and Wyoming. Some of the largest animals that ever lived– dinosaurs such as brontosaurus and allosaurus–left their tracks along the sea's muddy shores.

What will tomorrow's seas and oceans look like? Scientists believe that the Red Sea of Africa is the beginning of a new ocean. Its widest point is about 250 miles across, but its floor is spreading at almost one inch per year. Perhaps millions of years from now there will be one giant ocean again. What sort of creatures do you imagine will populate that future sea?

Weird ancestral creatures lurked
in the waters of Panthalassa.

Whirlpools

One of the world's most famous whirlpools is on one side of the Straits of Messina, between Italy and Sicily. Ancient sailors thought it was caused by a monster named Charybdis (kuh·RIB·dis). According to Greek legend, another monster, Scylla (SIL·uh), waited on the other side of the strait to gobble up sailors who were trying to avoid the swirling waters of the whirlpool. It was not an easy choice for the sailors. Scylla was a twelve-foot-tall monster with six heads, and each head had a wide mouth filled with a triple row of shark's teeth. Around the monster's waist were the snarling heads of vicious dogs. Charybdis was not as horrifying as Scylla in appearance. Still, his habit of drinking the ocean water and then spewing it out three times a day caused serious navigational problems for the ancient sailors.

Of course, these colorful creatures do not exist, but whirlpools do. The horrible funnel of the legend actually is a circular current, caused when the rising and falling tides squeeze back and forth through a deep, narrow strait.

Whirlpools can be found in many parts of the world. There are at least fifty off the coast of Norway alone. The strongest is called the maelstrom (MALE·strum). Sailors say the thundering sound of the maelstrom can be heard three miles away. The currents reach speeds of seven miles an hour, or nearly twice as fast as the fastest human swimmer. Strong local winds make navigation here even more difficult.

The swirling current of a whirlpool threatens a small boat.

Snow

Glacier

Land

Evaporation

Icebergs

Ocean

Floating Ice

Water has a unique trait—unlike most other substances, it expands when it freezes. Because of this, ice is lighter than water and it floats. The North Pole is located on a huge floating raft of ice in the Arctic Ocean. In 1958 the USS *Nautilus,* a nuclear-powered submarine, traveled from the Pacific Ocean to the Atlantic Ocean, *under* the polar ice. The following year, the USS *Skate* made a similar trip but broke through the ice at precisely the location of the North Pole, making it the first ship to actually "land" there.

Floating ice may form in arctic regions, but it can be found in other places. Huge floating chunks of ice, or icebergs, have been sighted near such unlikely tropical places as Bermuda and Rio de Janeiro. Arctic icebergs form when packed snow becomes a solid block of ice, called a glacier (GLAY·sher), which slides slowly toward the sea. When it reaches the water, a ragged chunk may break away and float out to sea as an iceberg. Between 10,000 and 15,000 icebergs are created every year. Some tower as high above the surface of the ocean as a thirty-story building. The tallest iceberg ever sighted was some 550 feet high, and just think—only about one-tenth of an iceberg is visible above the surface.

In Antarctica, a huge sheet of ice more than two miles thick covers the continent. Flat-topped icebergs form when a chunk of the ice splits away. Once, an iceberg twice the size of the whole state of Connecticut was sighted near Antarctica. Smaller icebergs that break away from such large ones are playfully called "bergy bits" and are about the size of a house.

Floating icebergs, most of which remain
hidden under the water's surface.

sea fan

shark

butterflyfish

starfish

coral

Coral Reefs

What is the greatest structure ever built on Earth? The Great Wall of China? The pyramids of Egypt? Believe it or not, the greatest structure on Earth wasn't built by humans. It is the Great Barrier Reef of Australia, built by billions of little sea creatures, each about the size of a pencil eraser. These amazing sea architects are called coral polyps (POL·ups).

Each tiny polyp lives in a cuplike shell that is connected to others shells of its kind. As each polyp dies, another polyp attaches itself to the empty shell, creating layers of hard shell over time. In this way, these tiny creatures build a stony wall of coral called a reef.

Special plants called algae (AL·jee) grow on the coral. They produce the oxygen needed by the polyp. The algae are so small that nearly 140 billion can live on just one square foot of living coral. Like most plants, the helpful algae need sunlight to survive. That is why most living corals are found in clear seawater at the top layer of a reef, within 150 feet of the surface.

At 1,250 miles long and up to 100 miles wide, the Great Barrier Reef is the largest coral reef in the world, but it isn't the only one. Coral reefs often form along the shoreline of a continent or around tropical islands, where the water is shallow and warm.

Coral polyps aren't the only tenants of a reef. Colorful parrotfish, graceful butterflyfish, spiny sea urchins, and hundreds of other creatures make their home there. Even the majestic shark patrols nearby looking for a likely meal.

Many creatures find shelter and food in the colorful coral reef.

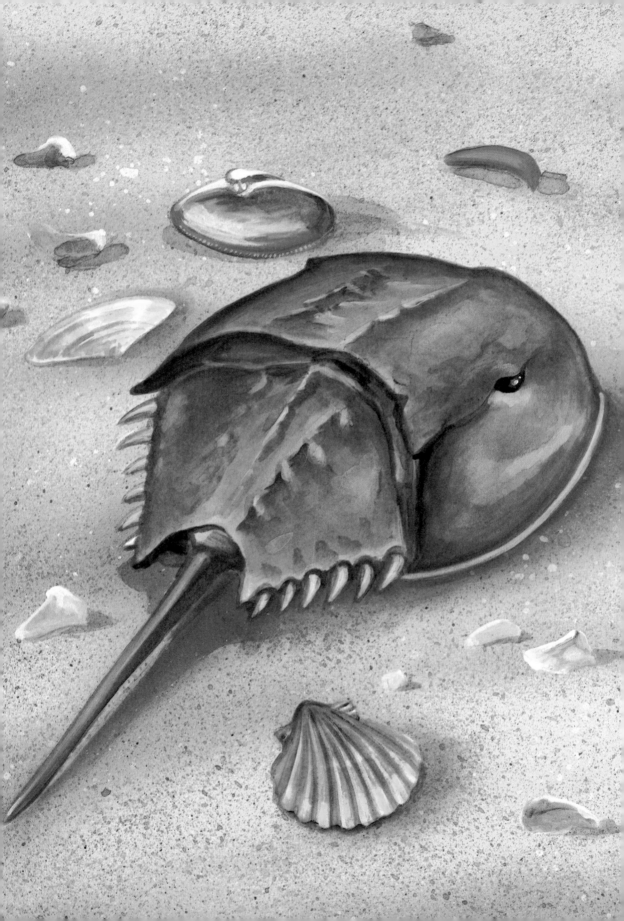

The Horseshoe Crab

The bizarre-looking horseshoe crab was already ancient when dinosaurs roamed the Earth. It has barely changed in the past 360 million years.

This animal's name is partly right and partly wrong: It is horseshoe-shaped but not a crab. A seagoing relative of spiders and scorpions, the horseshoe crab has many interesting features. To begin with, it has five pairs of legs and nine eyes. Four are true eyes. The rest are actually tiny light receptors under the shell. The crab's long hard tail looks dangerous but it isn't a weapon. When a strong wave sends it tumbling onto its back, the animal uses its handy tail as a lever to help flip itself over. Horseshoe crabs are not good swimmers, though. They crawl slowly along the ocean bottom, rarely wandering far from home.

During breeding season, hundreds of thousands of these animals creep up on the beach at Delaware Bay on the Atlantic coast of the United States. When a female crawls ashore at low tide, a male grasps her with his claws and ends up being towed along for the ride. She digs a hole in the sand and lays up to 10,000 tiny eggs, which the male then fertilizes. Gulls and sandpipers eat many of the eggs, but most remain under the sand until they hatch and the high tide washes them out to sea.

This unlikely creature may be a great help to humans. The blood of the horseshoe crab clots quickly when it comes in contact with endotoxins (EN·doh·tok·suns), a family of poisons produced by bacteria. Scientists use this animal's blood to test for endotoxins in medicines being developed for human use.

*The horseshoe crab—ancient and
strange relative of the scorpion.*

27

The Giant Squid

Because of its long wavy arms and huge size, the giant squid is probably the model for many tales of sea monsters. It can be fifty feet long, as big as a bus, and weigh up to forty-two tons—or more than *five* buses. Amazingly, a live giant squid has never been seen.

The giant squid is actually a mollusk, like snails and clams. However, this enormous mollusk has several unusual features. Unlike most mollusks, the squid doesn't have a shell. It has eight thick arms and two long slender ones, called tentacles (TEN·ta·kulz). The eight arms are lined with sucker disks, which hold prey like suction cups. The huge eyes of the giant squid—each the size of a Frisbee—move independently of each other. These strange eyes can be turned so that the creature can even see behind itself.

The remarkable squid has a wonderful way of traveling—it is jet-propelled. Strong muscles in the mantle (the top portion of the squid) suck water into the mantle cavity. These same muscles squirt the water out through a funnel. This propels the squid headfirst through the water as fast as thirty-two miles per hour.

The only known enemy of the giant squid is the huge sperm whale. These whales have been caught with squid tentacles thirty feet long in their stomachs and with scars left by squid suckers on their skins. One whale even had these scars *inside* its body. The squid seems to have continued to fight even after it was swallowed.

The squid has a few other tricks up its many sleeves. When threatened it can change its color or pattern, blending in with its background. If this doesn't work, the squid gives off an inky fluid and hides in the dark cloud.

As it battles the sperm whale, the giant squid releases an inky cloud.

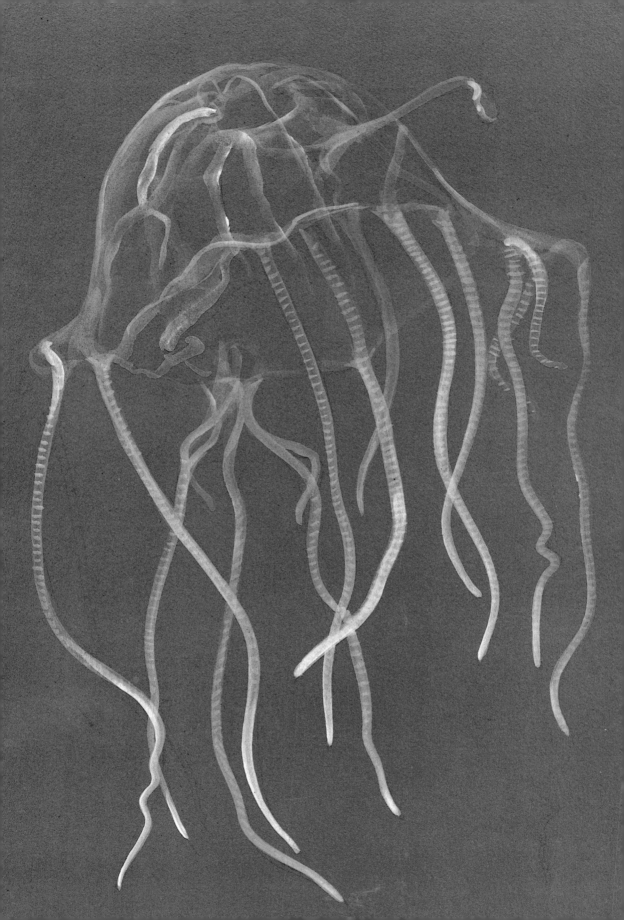

The Sea Wasp

The delicate sea wasp is a graceful jellyfish that drifts slowly near the surface of the sea. It is also the most poisonous sea creature known to humans. Its slender tentacles, each six to twenty feet long, stream out behind like filmy ribbons. This jellyfish doesn't swim after its prey—it just waits until something bumps into it. It can sting a human to death within five minutes. In fact, in the past twenty-five years, many more people swimming off the northern Australian coast have been killed by the sea wasp than by sharks.

In spite of its name, this animal doesn't sting like a wasp. It has special cells with tiny structures inside called nematocysts (nuh·MAT·oh·sists). Thin tubes in the cells have hooks that snag the victim's skin. Several poisons immediately flow through the tube and into the wound. One of them can stop a human heart in about three minutes. Another poison causes breathing to stop, and another causes red blood cells to burst. Imagine how poisonous just one sea wasp is. It can have up to sixty tentacles, each up to twenty feet long and each holding millions of stinging cells. Strangely enough, if the nematocysts are cut away from a jellyfish, they are still able to sting. One scientist found this out in a most unusual way. He performed an experiment that required chopping up some jellyfish tentacles. Small pieces of tentacle caught on his sleeve and dried. Months later, he happened to wear the same lab coat he had worn during the first experiment. When he accidently got the sleeve wet, the amazing nematocysts revived and stung him several times on his wrist.

The tentacles of the sea wasp have
millions of deadly stinging cells.

The Coelacanth

The coelacanth (SEEL·uh·kanth) first appeared on Earth
at least 350 million years ago. When scientists discovered
remains of this odd fish, they knew they had found a very
ancient form of creature. They were certain it had been
extinct for at least fifty million years. Then one day in 1938 an
amazing thing happened near the Comoro Islands, off the
east coast of Africa. A fisherman had found a coelacanth in
his net and it was very much alive. Over millions of years the
fish seemed to have changed very little from its ancestors.
Scientists were thrilled, because it gave them a firsthand look
at what prehistoric fish were really like. They offered rewards
for any other coelacanth specimens. Soon thereafter, some
other fishermen caught several more in deep water near the
islands. It seems the island natives had known about this fish
for a long time and even ate it dried and salted.

A little larger than its ancestors, the modern coelacanth
is about five feet long and weighs up to 160 pounds. It isn't a
very attractive fish. No one is sure what the coelacanth eats,
but it has a mouth full of large, sharp, widely spaced teeth. Its
rough scales form a heavy, protective armor, and there are
stiff spines in its fins. In fact, it was given the name *coelacanth*
(Greek for "hollow spine") because of its tough, spiny fins.
At the end of its wide tail there is another small, stubby tail.

The coelacanth is living proof that there are still things
to be discovered in the sea. Perhaps it isn't the only survivor
from the past. Perhaps, too, other incredible creatures are just
waiting to be discovered.

*The coelacanth–little changed
in over 350 million years.*

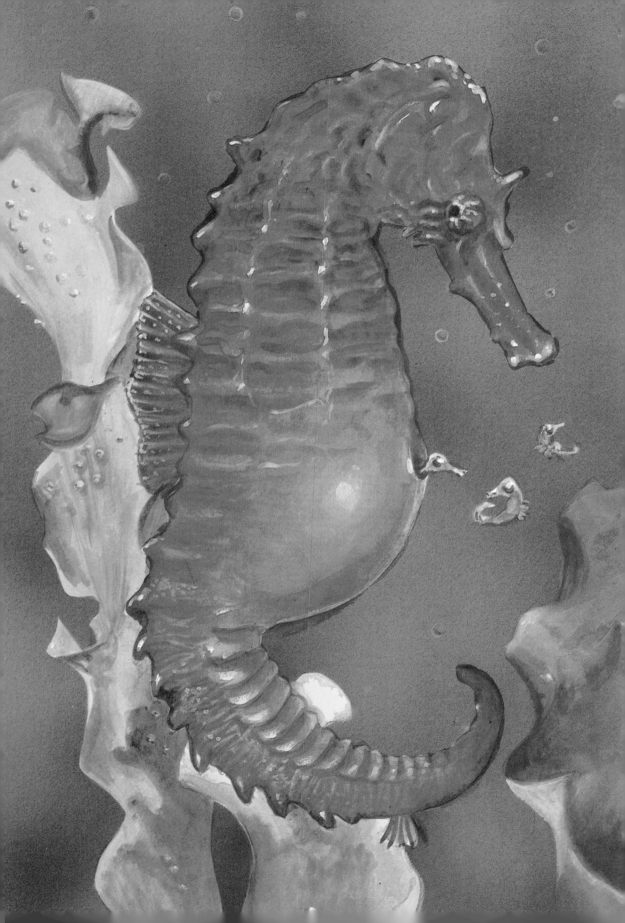

The Sea Horse

Have you ever heard of an armor-covered animal with the head of a horse, the tail of a monkey, and a pouch like a kangaroo's? Strange as it may seem, this is a description of the amazing sea horse.

The sea horse is a most unusual fish. Instead of scales, it is covered with a tough, ridged armor. Its head looks like that of a tiny horse, with a small mouth at the end of its tubelike snout. As for its tail, no other fish in the sea has one like that of the sea horse. This little animal can wrap its remarkable tail around a piece of seaweed much as a monkey wraps its tail around a tree branch. Another unusual feature of this odd, five-inch-tall fish is that it swims in an upright position. Since its fins are small and thin, however, the sea horse is not a very strong swimmer.

The strangest thing about the sea horse is the way it cares for its eggs. The female lays her eggs in a pouch on the male's tummy and then swims away. Several females may visit a male until his pouch is full. The eggs soon hatch, but the tiny babies are not developed enough to leave the pouch. When they are at last ready to exit, the father squeezes them out. Newborn sea horses are less than one-quarter-inch long and look exactly like their parents. As many as 300 sea horses can be born at one time.

A strange sight—newborn sea horses exiting their father's pouch.

The Wobbegong

If you were to draw a picture of a shark, you would probably color the animal gray or tan—but not if you were drawing the wobbegong (WAH·bee·gong). Looking more like an oriental rug than a fish, it is one of the most colorful sharks in the sea. In fact, it belongs to a group of animals called carpet sharks. The fantastic patterns on the wobbegong's skin camouflage the shark among the shadows of shallow, rocky reefs. Weedlike, fleshy fringe along its wide mouth completes its disguise. The wobbegong is so well hidden that it only has to wait until an unsuspecting crab or fish wanders too close. The shark quickly snaps up and gobbles down its meal, then waits quietly for the next course.

Nicknamed the wobby, this animal is not usually aggressive, but it will bite if annoyed or stepped on. It has several rows of sharp teeth and is known to hang on stubbornly. In 1788, the first English settlers in Australia were amazed by the wobbegong. In Sydney Cove, a fisherman left a wobbegong on a dock in the hot sun for over two hours. When a small dog ran up to sniff at it, the shark immediately grasped the dog's leg in it jaws. Nearby sailors had to help the dog to break free. Another wobbegong bit a diver and wouldn't let go, even when stabbed with a knife. The diver's companion was able to pry the shark's jaws apart, and the two men towed the animal to their boat. As the diver climbed aboard, the shark bit him again and held on tightly. Once again, his companion had to pry the shark loose.

Fantastic colors and fleshy fringe—
the wobbegong's trademark.

Cruising Fish

What's that in the air? Is it a bird? A plane? No, it's a fish. At least forty different kinds of flying fish are found in warm waters all around the world. They rarely grow more than eighteen inches long and most are smaller. A flying fish does not "flap" as birds do. It glides through the air by holding its pectoral (PEK·tor·al) or "chest" fins on either side of its body, like the wings of an airplane. The amazing Atlantic flying fish has very long pectoral fins. These make for a very large "wingspan" when flying. When the fish is swimming, the fins fold back against the body, almost reaching the tail. The California flying fish has four "wings." In flight, it uses the pectoral fins and another pair just below these, called the pelvic (PEL·vik) fins, to glide for hundreds of feet.

The flying fish is a strong swimmer and spends most of its time in the water. When threatened, however, this unusual creature will fly above the water to escape its enemies, which include the speedy dolphin and the dangerous swordfish. For its "takeoff," the flying fish swims very fast toward the surface. Just as its head leaves the water, the fish beats its powerful tail very quickly. Once above the surface, it spreads its fins and glides low in the air for up to 650 feet. As it sinks back toward the surface, the silvery fish flutters its forked tail in the water, which allows it to leap into the air for an even longer flight. The incredible flying fish can reach air speeds of up to thirty-five miles per hour, make several leaps in a row, and even turn in the air.

*Using pectoral fins, a flying fish cruises
in the air while another takes off.*

Grunion

The California grunion (GRUN·yun) is a little fish that has an exceptional way of protecting its eggs from predators of the sea: It lays its eggs on land. Between March and August, when the weather and tides are just right, the grunion lays its eggs in the darkness of night. This happens three or four nights a month, after either the full moon or the new moon, and then only for a few hours after high tide.

The grunion gathering or "run" begins as a few lone scouts ride the incoming tide onto the beach. Within a short time, thousands of these silvery six-inch-long fish may be flopping and sliding about on the sand. Accompanied by up to eight males, each female wriggles her tail into the wet sand until she is buried nearly halfway. In this hole she lays about 2,000 eggs. The males fertilize the eggs and slip back to the sea, and the female squirms out of the sand and follows. The grunion may be out of the water for several minutes, but the egg-laying process takes less than one minute.

The eggs remain buried deep in the moist sand for about ten days, until the next high tide washes them free. The young, called fry, hatch within two or three minutes and are carried out to sea. The one-quarter-inch-long fry are able to swim immediately. If the eggs are not uncovered by the first high tide, they can survive up to two weeks. With luck, the next high tide will hatch the grunion and wash them to sea.

During the run, people are allowed on the beach to catch the tasty grunion, but there are some restrictions. You must have a fishing license and you cannot use nets. You have to catch the slippery grunion with your bare hands.

A gathering of grunions coming
ashore to breed at high tide.

Electric eel

Electric Eels and Rays

Can you imagine a fish that can produce enough electricity to run a blender? The South American electric eel is such a fish. It can also discharge enough electricity to kill a swimmer up to ten feet away. This freshwater dweller's name is misleading, however. It is not an eel at all but a fish that is more closely related to the harmless little minnow.

The South American electric eel can grow up to eight feet long and weigh about ninety pounds. Up to half of its weight is in its electricity-producing organs. These highly specialized organs are made up of disklike cells arranged in columns. In a very large electric eel there may be a million of these cells or more. The electric eel may use its special ability to defend itself or to stun prey. There is another possible use, too. This unusual fish sends out electrical signals that encircle it in a special pattern, which changes when it touches something. In this way, the animal can "sense" the location of objects and find its way in muddy water.

There are about thirty different kinds of electric ray, also called numbfish. These ocean relatives of the shark are less powerful than electric eels, but they certainly can deliver an intense shock to stun prey and to protect themselves. Like most electric rays, the California torpedo ray often hides partly buried in sand on the seafloor. However, the torpedo ray is aggressive and will turn toward an attacker. With its tiny mouth open as if to bite, it will swim after a diver. That may be just a threat since torpedo rays are not known to bite, but most divers take the hint and leave them alone.

The electric California torpedo ray
calmly waits for prey to swim by.

Fish That Glow

The bottom of the sea is a dark place that sunlight doesn't reach. The waters are usually very cold, and plants cannot grow in this sunless world. It may seem impossible that animals can live here, but they do, and many actually glow in the dark. Like dim stars moving against the blackness of space, their light is a cool, steady glow. Pockets of bacteria in their skin glow by chemical reaction. The soft light helps certain fish to recognize each other or to attract prey.

The ocean bottom is home to many glow-in-the-dark fish. The anglerfish can live more than a mile below the surface. The female has a spine on her head that looks like a fishing rod with a tiny piece of glowing bait at the end. The wiggling light lures the angler's prey close enough for the tricky fish to swallow it down.

The foot-long viperfish is a scary sight. Its sharp teeth are curved back to hold squirming prey. These stabbing fangs are so long that the viperfish can't close its mouth. A thin spine with a glowing light on its tip trails along behind the spooky fish as it swims.

Have you ever heard someone say, "His eyes are bigger than his stomach"? This saying doesn't apply to the peculiar black swallower. As tiny patches of light on its side attract prey, the black swallower can open its jaws very wide. This amazing six-inch-long fish can swallow something two or three times its own size. It is able to move its backbone, gills, and even its heart aside to let the meal pass into its huge, flexible belly.

Glow-in-the-dark creatures lurk at
the very bottom of the sea.

Poisonous Fish

Fish have many different ways of protecting themselves from danger. Some bite. Others swim quickly away or burrow deep into the sand. Still other fish protect themselves from enemies in a very interesting way—with deadly poison. These venomous sea creatures are called scorpionfish.

Scorpionfish are among the most poisonous fish in the sea. Though not always deadly to humans, the wounds they cause are painful and slow to heal. There are about 300 kinds of scorpionfish in seas around the world. One member of this dangerous family, the six-inch-long lionfish, is one of the most beautiful fish to be found in the tropical ocean. Like an undersea peacock, it displays its delicately colored and patterned fins. It may be small and pretty, but this fish is equipped with eighteen poisonous spines.

The most harmful scorpionfish is the stonefish. It is as ugly as the lionfish is beautiful. Looking like a lumpy, weed-covered chunk of rock, it has scaleless, slimy skin. Incredibly tough, poisonous spines jut out of several fins on its back and near its tail. This ugly fish lies as still as a stone on the shallow sea bottom. When a small fish swims too near, the stonefish quickly gobbles it down. Since it stays so still and is very hard to see, the stonefish is likely to be stepped on by people wading in shallow water. The spines are so tough they can pierce the sole of a tennis shoe! The stab can kill a human within two hours. Even if the unlucky victim does not die, small doses of the poison can lead to the loss of a toe or foot.

The camouflaged lionfish is beautiful—but very poisonous.

Fish Out of Water

Someday, road signs that say "Fish Crossing" may be needed on Florida highways. Though not native to the state, a large population of walking catfish are doing very well there. These pale pink fish originally came all the way from Thailand. Pet suppliers stocked them in outdoor ponds to sell to aquarium owners as an oddity. The catfish seemed to have other ideas. They simply left the ponds and moved to wild waterways. Walking catfish are able to wriggle along on land, using their fins to push themselves forward. They can survive out of water for several hours. That's because a special organ in their head allows them to use oxygen directly from the air. These fish must stay moist, though, so they usually travel on land only at night or when it's raining.

The mudskipper is another type of fish that's at home in or out of the water. It lives in shallow, muddy mangrove swamps, eating tiny crabs and insects. When underwater, this plump, eight-inch-long fish swims very well. It can escape from a predator by burrowing into the soft swamp mud, but the mudskipper has an even more interesting way of staying out of danger. It can leave the water and move clumsily along on its pectoral fins. If the fish is in a hurry, it can "skip" along by curling and straightening its body. The amazing mudskipper can cover two feet in one leap.

The mudskipper is comfortable in— and out of—water.

The Emperor Penguin

The emperor penguin can survive temperatures far colder than any other animal can. This unusual bird lives in Antarctica, the coldest place on Earth. Here, temperatures often drop to eighty degrees below zero, but the majestic-looking emperor penguin has developed interesting ways to keep warm. First, the bird's odd suit of feathers helps it to stay warm in its icy home. The feathers are tiny and packed very close together, about seventy per square inch. They also overlap and are coated with oil to make them waterproof. The feathers hold an insulating layer of air next to the skin. A thick sheet of fat beneath its skin also helps to keep the penguin cozy.

Penguins cannot fly but they are excellent swimmers. Most can swim as fast as fifteen miles per hour. Emperor penguins, which are the largest in the penguin family, dive to depths of more than 900 feet to catch the small squid they like to eat.

The eggs of the emperor penguin are laid during the coldest months of the antarctic winter. During this time, the females each lay one large egg and leave to feed in the sea. While they are gone, the males protect the eggs. Each male holds an egg carefully on top of his feet. He has a flap of skin near his feet that covers the egg and helps to keep it warm. During this incubation period, large groups of males huddle close together with their backs to the freezing wind. They remain like that for about two months. Just as the eggs are hatching, the females return. Each thin, tired male eagerly places his tiny chick on its mother's feet and heads for the sea to search for food.

Antarctica, the coldest place on Earth,
is home to the emperor penguin.

The Narwhal

Have you ever seen pictures of a unicorn? It is a beautiful, mythical horse with a long, twisted horn jutting out from the center of its forehead. Perhaps the legend began when ancient sailors brought home the marvelous ivory tusk of an incredible whale called the narwhal (NAR·wall). Narwhals belong to a small group of whales that also includes the *beluga,* which is Russian for "white whale." Narwhals live in groups called pods in the cold arctic seas off Russia and Canada. The twelve- to sixteen-foot-long whale dives deep in the chilly waters to search for a meal of fish or crabs. It also dives to escape its natural enemies—polar bears, killer whales, and humans.

You may be surprised to learn that the narwhal's remarkable tusk is actually an overgrown tooth. Both the male and the female are born with two forward-pointing teeth in the upper jaw. As they grow older, the left tooth of only the male will pierce right through his upper lip. It grows in a twisting spiral that can reach a length of eight feet on a twelve-foot-long narwhal and weigh as much as twenty pounds. Hunters have captured whales with two tusks, but that is very rare.

The purpose of the famous tusk is a mystery. Some people think the narwhal uses it as a weapon or as a tool to punch holes in the ice. It's probably too brittle to use in either way, however. The tusk may be used to root tasty crabs and shrimp from the sandy seafloor. However, females manage to find their food without a tusk. Perhaps it's simply a decoration to attract a mate or threaten a rival. We may not be sure how the whale uses his uncommon tusk, but Eskimos have found it perfect for spears and tent poles.

The spiraling tusk of the narwhal
is a magical sight.

53

Salmon Migration

Perhaps the most remarkable journey of any creature on Earth is that of the salmon (SAM·un). Their journey begins in the fresh waters of rivers and streams, where salmon are born. They soon make their way downstream to the open ocean, where the fish will live out most of their lives. But when it is time to breed, the salmons' journey takes an amazing turn: No matter where they lived in the ocean, the salmon head for the streams where they were born.

The salmons' journey to their breeding grounds is often long. Sometimes their destination is hundreds of miles away, and they do not eat along the way. The longest journey recorded is 1,730 miles. That's like swimming more than halfway from Los Angeles to Honolulu.

Some salmon change appearance when it comes time to breed. The five-foot-long Pacific king salmon, the largest of its kind, turns a reddish color, and the males develop unusual hooked jaws. Thousands of these fish then head for the Yukon River where they were born.

The adventure is not over when the salmon finally reach their river. To find the exact spot where they will reproduce, or spawn, the salmon must swim upriver against incredible currents. Fishermen and hungry bears catch many of the salmon. The fish have been known to leap more than nine feet in the air to clear a barrier or avoid being caught.

Finally, weak and starved, the survivors arrive at their destination to breed. The female lays up to 14,000 eggs. Within a few days, however, both the male and female die. The young salmon hatch and soon begin their long trip to the ocean. Somehow they remember the place where they began, and someday they, too, will return.

A mature salmon struggles its way upstream toward home.

The Marine Iguana

When you think of a lizard you probably picture a creature
in a dense jungle or hot, dry desert. Have you ever heard of a
lizard that swims in the ocean? The mighty marine iguana
(ih·GWAN·uh) does just that. This peculiar four- to five-foot-
long lizard looks like it should be the star of a dinosaur
movie. It lives in huge colonies on the beaches of the
Galapagos Islands near Ecuador, South America.

The marine iguana begins its day by warming itself in
the early morning sun. Then it wriggles toward the huge
lava rocks on the island shoreline, which are covered with
slippery seaweed and algae. Powerful waves crash over the
marine iguana as it grazes on the plants. A strong wave may
sweep the animal into the water, but it isn't a problem for
this extraordinary lizard. With its legs tucked in, and with
powerful thrusts of its long tail, the marine iguana swims
very well. It can dive as deep as fifty feet to search for a meal,
easily staying underwater for ten minutes or more at a time.
In fact, this lizard actually drinks seawater. Special organs
remove the salt from its bloodstream.

The male marine iguana usually claims a small area as
his own and will fight to defend it from other males. During
breeding season, he develops colorful red patches on his
sides, and the spiky crest on his head turns green. Perhaps
this display makes him more attractive to females. It certainly
must get their attention. Sometimes two males fight over one
female, but the battle usually isn't serious. It often ends by
the winner bumping the loser off a rock into the sea.

*Lizard swimmers—huge and colorful
marine iguanas.*

The Journey of the Green Turtle

It's not so easy to figure out how the green turtle got its name. This three-foot-long sea turtle is not actually named for its yellowish-brown shell but for its bright green body fat. This green color comes from its food. The only sea turtle to eat only plants, this turtle grazes in shallow beds of sea grass, which reasonably enough is called turtle grass.

These creatures spend almost all of their lives in the warm oceans of the world. However, green sea turtles lay their eggs on land. To do this, they undertake an amazing and difficult journey back to the same beach where they were born. Some swim more than 1,400 miles to reach their breeding waters. However, the real work begins when the female turtle heads ashore. After breeding in the water, she drags herself onto the sand. This is no easy job, since she can weigh as much as 300 pounds. Far onto the beach, past where any wave can reach, she digs a hole with her back flippers. She lays up to 100 eggs and then covers her nest with sand. Finally, after much hard work, she returns to the sea.

When the young hatch, they must dig their way to the surface. Remarkably, the young turtles know the right direction to the ocean, even though they can't see which way that is. The race to the sea is very dangerous for the tiny hatchlings. Birds swoop down on them, and lizards swallow them up. If they are lucky enough to make it to the water, they may still be eaten by hungry fish. Those few that survive are not seen again until they arrive at the feeding grounds of their parents about a year later. Where they have been and how they have survived remain a mystery.

A green sea turtle hovers over a bed of turtle grass.

sun star

blood starfish

green sea urchin shells

purple sea urchin

sand dollar

Echinoderms

Echinoderms (eh·KINE·oh·dermz), or spiny-skinned animals, include some of the most unusual creatures of the ocean: starfish, sea urchins, and sand dollars.

Starfish come in a rainbow of colors, from deep purple to bright yellow and red. Some are as large as three feet wide, but others are as small as a dime. Most have five arms lined with many tiny, suckerlike feet that help them cling to rocks, even in stormy surf. A starfish often uses its feet to pry open oysters. Pulling the shell apart a little with its sucker disks, it squeezes a bit of its own stomach lining inside. The stomach fluid irritates the prey, causing the oyster to open wider. The starfish can then shove more of its stomach inside the shell and digest the animal. A large group of sea stars can destroy an oyster bed overnight.

Sea urchins look like prickly pin cushions. They "walk" slowly along on their stiff spines. The sea urchin's mouth is on the underside of its shell. It has five sharp teeth for grazing on algae along the rocks or sand. Some sea urchins may be as large as ten inches in diameter.

Sand dollars are found on smooth, sandy ocean floor. They are covered with rough, short spines and tiny, hairlike projections, called cilia (SIL·ee·uh). The sand dollar waves the cilia to trap microscopic sea creatures called plankton on its shell. The cilia move the plankton slowly toward the sand dollar's mouth on the underside of the shell. Starfish sometimes eat sand dollars. When a starfish is nearby, sand dollars escape by burrowing deeply into the sand.

Very colorful echinoderms—starfish,
sea urchins, and sand dollars.

The Future of Our Oceans

When you look out over the enormous ocean, it seems almost impossible that humankind could affect it. However, scientists who study the ocean are learning that man's interactions with the sea can make a difference. It's up to us whether or not this difference will be harmful.

Since ancient times people have fished the sea. Our ancestors took very little, but modern fishermen catch millions of tons of fish every year. As a result, some species' very existence is endangered. The amount taken of any one kind of fish must therefore be carefully monitored, even limited. This way we can be sure there will always be enough fish left for them to reproduce.

Offshore oil wells are becoming a familiar sight. They provide much of the oil we need. Unfortunately, about 200,000 tons of oil are accidentally spilled into the ocean every year. For many years we have also dumped garbage and other wastes in the oceans, thinking that these would settle far out to sea. Actually, the strong ocean currents have carried the oil and wastes everywhere, exposing sea plants and animals to dangerous chemicals. These wastes can kill ocean life, ruin the underwater environment for years, and make beaches unclean and unsafe for swimmers.

No one owns the ocean. It belongs to all of us, and we are all responsible for its care. That's a big job and a very important one. People in all countries must cooperate. By working together, we can protect and preserve for the future our oceans and the creatures that live there.

For Further Reading

Armour, Richard: *Strange Monsters of the Sea*, New York City, McGraw-Hill, 1979.

Berrill, Jacqueline, and Berrill, N.J.: *1001 Questions Answered About the Seashore*, New York City, Dover Books, 1976.

Blair, Carvel Hall: *Exploring the Sea*, New York City, Random House, 1986.

Bunting, Eve: *The Giant Squid*, Englewood Cliffs, New Jersey, Julian Messner, 1981.

Barle, Olive L.: *Strange Fishes of the Sea*, New York City, Morrow Junior Books, 1968.

Jacobs, Francine: *The Sargasso Sea*, New York City, William Morrow and Co., 1975.

Raymo, Chet: *The Crust of Our Earth*, New York City, Prentice Hall, 1983.

Rockell, Bernard W.: *Whales and Dolphins*, New York City, Puffin Books, 1975.

Seddon, Tony, and Bailey, Jill: *The Living World*, New York City, Doubleday, 1986.

Simon, Seymour: *Strange Creatures*, New York City, Four Winds Press, 1981.

Index